Microfinance in Sub-Saharan Africa

Microfinance in Sub-Saharan Africa
Responding to the Voices of Poor People

Irene Banda Mutalima

regnum
Mini Book
Series

First published 2022 by Regnum Books International

Regnum is an imprint of the Oxford Centre for Mission Studies
St. Philip and St. James Church
Woodstock Road, Oxford OX2 6HR, UK
www.regnumbooks.net

09 08 07 06 05 04 03 7 6 5 4 3 2 1

British Library Cataloguing in Publication Data. A catalogue record for this book is available from the British Library.

ISBN: 978-1-5064-9750-1
eBook ISBN: 978-1-5064-9751-8

Typeset in Candara by Words by Design.

Photo by Bilal O. on Unsplash

The publication of this volume is made possible through the financial assistance of Evangelisches Missionswerk.

Distributed by 1517 Media in the US, Canada, India, and Brazil

Contents

Abbreviations

Abbreviations

COSUN – Community Support for the Needy

CPSCC – Chipata Pamodzi Savings and Credit Cooperative

PROSPECT – Programme of Support for Poverty Elimination and Community Transformation: a CARE International project

We are Strong, but ...
– Women Working for Food

I was meeting with the sixteen women who are members of the Community Support for the Needy (COSUN) group located in one of the squatter settlements of Lusaka, Zambia. The group was formed to participate in the various activities meant to improve their livelihoods. Their local leaders had selected them to be part of my participatory action research project, which was exploring ways of responding to poor people's voices with microfinance. The women are reminiscing about the times when they did manual work: how they performed feats they were not prepared for, in the early '90s.

Jenala is one of the women. *Twalikosa ifwe* (we are strong), she says, with some dejection on her face. She is describing how they participated in the food-for-work programme in their settlement. In exchange for their labour, the women would receive essential foodstuffs that include a bag of maize meal (used to prepare Zambia's staple food, known by different names like *nshima*, *buhobe* or *bwali*), a bottle of cooking oil and some dry rations. This was often what the women needed as food supplies for their families. The women accepted the food-for-work programme as one way they could support their families. However, these memories were not all pleasant.

Part of the work the women did included clearing drainages, creating a road network and preparing for water points. Jenala does not mince her words as she expresses her disappointment that they did backbreaking work with very little reward.

> Balatubomfyafye kwati tuli ma tools. Balebonfya abantu – ukubapafye ubunga, but balebomba hard job, ukwimba umufolo ... inchito ishakosa.[1]

Lubuto is one of the women who picks up the discussion thread:

> Like it has been said, we are just left behind. We are strong and we want to work, but we do not have anyone to help us develop, to tell us what to do. Even doing business requires someone to teach you. We do not have such a person.

Sonaya and Jenala add:

> Sonaya: They use us who are not educated because we are ignorant.

> Jenala: ... we are talking about what we see from our leaders who use us.

As part of a CARE International project, the women had been tasked to dig trenches for laying of water pipes, clear land portions in readiness for road works and remove rubbish dumps that had

---

[1] *They use us the way they use tools. They used people – hard work of digging drainages and other strenuous jobs for a bag of mealie meal.* Bemba is one of the local languages used in Lusaka. Future quotations will also be in English in the main text.

accumulated over years, thereby posing a health threat. This was back-breaking work but the women were determined, even when required to remove large rocks. They knew that they would get food as payment – this was the deal. Their complaints stem from their perception that they were not receiving what was due to them commensurate with the labour effort they put in.

The Squatter Settlements

This settlement where the women were located was one of many such settlements in Zambia that housed indigenous people who had come to work in the mines or among the white settlers. At the turn of the twentieth century, the Private Locations Ordinance of 1939 enabled people who moved into the urban centres to stay on and not return to their villages of origin. The enactment of the African Housing Ordinance in 1948 gave permission to African labourers to bring their families into the towns or cities they worked in.[2] Most Africans who opted to remain after the expiration of employment contracts settled in squatter settlements where they put up dwellings as they could afford. "The striking feature of the early self-help housing ... was the use of unconventional building materials and their location just outside the city/town boundary. The Private Locations Ordinance ... did not insist on the statutory building standards."[3] Thus began the squatter settlements.

---

[2] E. Mutale, *Management of Urban Development in Zambia* (Hants, England: Ashgate, 2004).

[3] Mulenga, C.L. 2003, 'The Case of Lusaka', Zambia Institute of Economic and Social Research, University of Zambia, Lusaka http://www.ucl.ac.uk/dpu-projects/Global_Report/pdfs/Lusaka.pdf accessed on 12th Sept 2013

Without government support for necessary amenities like sanitation and roads, squatter settlements suffered environmental pollution and an increase in diseases due to lack of social amenities. In 1981, the World Bank commissioned the Lusaka Squatter Upgrading and Sites and Services Project, which "was probably the first upgrading scheme in Sub-Saharan Africa and provided more than 30,000 new and improved shelter sites in informal settlements in the city."[4] Residents of these squatter settlements cited problems such as "illegality of residence and the general lack of water, school, roads, sewerage/drainage/sanitation, security, building space, clinic, community centre, employment ... "[5] Poverty was rampant and the local authorities did not have resources to address the problems but sought to partner with the donor community to find solutions. Donors and the NGO community took on the role of supporting improvements in infrastructure, services, the environment and generally the quality of life in the settlements.[6]

Poverty in Squatter Settlements

Zambia's economic success had for a long time been driven on the back of copper production – thus, the fall of copper prices in 1974 and the oil shock of the 1970s spelled a serious decline in the economy, leaving Zambia near the bottom of the World Bank's

---

[4] World Bank, *Upgrading Low-Income Urban Settlements – Zambia Country Assessment Report* (Washington, USA 2002), p. 13.

[5] World Bank, *Upgrading*, p. 10.

[6] J. Garrett, 'Community Empowerment and Scaling up in Urban Areas', FCND discussion paper 177 (Washington: International Food Policy Research Institute, 2004). http://ebrary.ifpri.org/utils/getfile/collection/p15738coll2/id/75799/filename/75721.pdf accessed on 14th March 2016.

hierarchy of developing nations.[7] The economic decline eroded many of the benefits of living in urban areas, resulting in very high levels of poverty. By 1993, 73.8% of the Zambian population was below the poverty line. The Zambian government partnered with the World Food Programme and commissioned the Peri-Urban Self Help Project to implement a food-for-work project. CARE International took on the responsibility of supervising the implementation of the project.[8] In 1994 CARE adapted the sustainable livelihoods approach, which focused on sustainable access to income through various resources such as food, potable water, health facilities, educational opportunities and housing through community participation and social integration.[9]

Local government facilitated the establishment of community-based organisations whose mandate included overseeing improvements to market facilities, roads, drainage, water, sanitation and garbage collection, as well as promoting economic and cultural activities. The project started with the food-for-work component and evolved into community-driven interventions that would reduce poverty through community-based and self-managed financial services society groups. The groups would pool together savings and lend to one another for business purposes. This variation of microfinance would self-manage based on the traditional savings system commonly known as *chilimba*.[10]

---

[7] Rakner, L. 2003, 'Political and Economic Liberalisation in Zambia 1991-2001', The Nordic Africa Institute, Sweden.

[8] Garrett, 'Community Empowerment'.

[9] Frankenberger, T.R., Drinkwater, M. and Maxwell, D. 2000: 'Operationalizing Household Livelihood Security: A Holistic Approach for Addressing Poverty and Vulnerability.' CARE USA.

[10] Garrett, 'Community Empowerment', p. 16.

The microfinance component placed financial services society groups under the oversight of newly formed community umbrella cooperatives, whose role included managing a pool of funds available for group members to borrow from. One such cooperative was the Chipata Pamodzi Savings and Credit Cooperative (CPSCC). COSUN was started as a financial services society under the oversight of CPSCC.

Against this background, the COSUN women recognised CARE International as their great benefactor in these projects. While recognising CARE's magnanimity, the women speculate that the help only ended with bringing them water and not much else that would improve their lives. This is what they had to say:

> Sonaya: *We know that CARE brought us water, but after that there was nothing else we saw.*

> Jenala: *... they [CARE] wanted to teach us how we can develop our homes.*

> Pelile: *... CARE brought development but we only saw water.*

> Pelile: *... there is no other project that they thought to fund.*

The women identify poverty as their big problem. They are not able to buy food over sustained periods, send their children to school or have proper housing. Ultimately, they find it impossible to manage their homes. One of them reported that she is "unable to think properly" when she does not know where to turn. Their efforts do not seem to bring them anywhere closer to solutions that would ameliorate their poverty status. They listed these problems:

> *Poverty is deprivation.*
> *Poverty means suffering.*
> *Poverty means not having enough food.*
> *Poverty means failing to meet the needs of the home.*
> *Poverty is being helpless because of not having money.*
> *Poverty is one thing that causes a person to stop thinking properly – it is being deprived.*
> *Poverty is disease in the home, hunger and children not going to school.*
> *I have failed to build my house because of not having money.*

For these women, life had not really improved. As they look back, they wonder whether even the food they received was proportionate to the labour they provided. Jenala remembers an elderly lady who toiled with everybody else and received *some mealie-meal and a bit of cooking oil.* They seem to lay the blame on the local leaders that had been appointed by CARE International to distribute and supervise the work equitably in exchange for the food. It is by these leaders that the women feel cheated. The women feel that these leaders used them for little or no benefit – they perceive that they suffer vulnerabilities in relation to the leadership meant to help them.

As a financial services society group they have limited understanding of what it all means. Though they make regular savings and deposits with CPSCC, the women have no record of the savings they made over time and therefore cannot hold the CPSCC leaders accountable. They also have not been able to access credit due to lack of funds with CPSCC. During the research, a conversation between the women and Chiseche, the CPSCC officer, reveals the women's knowledge gaps regarding how the loan scheme works:

> Mwaba: *So you give loans from the money that we bring here as savings? I am asking ... maybe some of you have been paid something ... I have never been paid.*

> Pelile: *Does it mean that all the groups who make savings bring the money here [to the cooperative]? Then you take that money and give it out as loans?*

> Sonaya: *Yes, that is what they give us as loans.*

> Voices: *We did not know.*

During this meeting, the women learn from the CPSCC representative that they are entitled to 10% interest on their savings. This was not common knowledge though:

> Sonaya: *We said we do not know anything because this girl said that the cooperative pays ten percent through the group.*

> Towa: *Sometime back ... at the end of the year, they used to give us ... now I don't know whether this is happening as she says ... maybe 5 or 4 years have passed since we were given.*

> Kunda: *Maybe the problem is that savings have come down ... so there is no money to give us. How will they give us interest? But in past years, they used to give us.*

I recall that, when I embarked on this part of the research, I met with the CPSCC leaders for introductions to the women. The CPSCC leaders were quick to recognise that the cooperative provided a place where the community voices could be heard, though it was also clear that they did not seem to have a clear and sustainable way of achieving this in the absence of the donor who set them up continuing funding support. With dwindling loan funds they saw their role diminishing, as they were unable to offer loans, though they continued to collect savings from faithful groups like COSUN. Boniface, a board member with CPSCC, explained:

> *We used to have a lot of groups and CARE used to work with us. I think it has all to do with the manner CARE left. They just left without leaving what I call an exit strategy. They more like just left people in suspense ... and the moment CARE left, people used to come here expecting that CARE left some money.*

The establishment of CPSCC was part of the exit strategy that CARE activated to enable community structures to continue with interventions that were in place. However, this strategy was fraught with leadership and funding challenges. Interestingly, despite the challenges, the leaders still commanded respect and influence on those that looked up to them, like the COSUN women. When planning for this research, they were able to nominate the COSUN group to participate. As part of the research, the women would inform the process of lending them money that would support business undertakings to create earnings.

As the research progressed, when the CPSCC leaders realised that the promised loans to the women would materialise, they called for a side meeting with the intention of having the loan money go through the CPSCC offices. At this point, the women exercised their voice and objected to this requirement. The CPSCC leaders were infuriated and "washed their hands" of the COSUN women. They informed the COSUN women that they would no longer support them.

It was important for the COSUN women to participate in this research that aimed to explore how to respond to the voices of poor people with microfinance services. Poverty reduction through microfinance is tied to the belief that access to credit enables poor people to increase business earnings and improve livelihoods. The Church has often embraced microfinance as part of its theology of social transformation. Microfinance practitioners have therefore carried the burden of managing their institutions and ensuring improvements in poor people's lives – a complex combination given that livelihood changes can only be confirmed by people experiencing poverty.

Working with the COSUN group as part of the research aimed to respond to the research questions:

1a. What are poor people's voices about their livelihoods?

1b. How do those voices influence actions that contribute to their livelihood needs?

The following chapter will describe the research process.

Research Structure

The goal of this research was to find ways in which poor people could inform an effective design and delivery of financial services that benefit them. I therefore purposed to create dialogue space to engage those voices. The first inquiry point was to understand poor people's cultural-historic context that enables their voices to influence beneficial actions, then provide microfinance loans informed by those voices. This required two things to happen:

Identify communities that would willingly participate in the research.

Identify a research process that would enable those outcomes.

Identifying Research Communities

The research included the participation of the women of the Chinyika community in Tavengwa village in Gutu District of rural Zimbabwe and women of the COSUN group of Chipata squatter settlement in urban Lusaka, Zambia. I knew the communities through my work contacts.

At the time that I was Executive Director of Ecumenical Church Loan Fund International in Switzerland, the traditional leader of the Chinyika community requested our microfinance services for his community. They had successfully attained food security by working together despite the famine caused by persistent drought. Their cultural and historical connection to the land and traditional grain crops informed decisions that led to securing a food security solution. Their story was a significant component in locating the efficacy of poor people's voices.

In early years, I had been part of a team that designed the community-driven microfinance initiative for CARE International in Zambia. I was therefore aware of the existence of community cooperative societies that participated in this initiative. I knew that there would be experiences of poor people interacting and possibly informing microfinance activities. I approached the Chipata Pamodzi Savings and Credit Cooperative (CPSCC) leaders, who recommended that the research be conducted with COSUN, one of their savings and credit groups.

In both communities, my goal was to create an atmosphere of trust and mutual respect. Having secured permission from community leaders, I outlined the purpose of the research and the procedure to be taken to secure their willing and un-coerced participation.

Identifying a Research Process

I chose *participatory action research* as the methodology that would allow me to research, develop and implement a new approach to lending money to poor people in response to financing needs that meet their livelihood aspirations.

Understanding Participatory Action Research

Participatory action research is a reflective process whose primary aim is to achieve change and new knowledge. The participation of local people in research recognises their expertise in resolving their problems and evolving solutions. Action research has been used to emancipate oppressed people, and acts on social policies and practices that create inequality. Participation is based on the continuing belief that a "bottom-up" approach empowers participants to become agents of change and decision-making. This also implies that resources stand a better chance of being used appropriately while including poor people's voices. Participation can therefore break dependence on external providers, as communities become masters of their own development. Voluntary participation in a climate of mutual trust enables participants to address contentious issues with few or no confrontations but without diluting the issues at hand. I was able to reach this level of mutual trust during the research with both communities.

Action research has several steps. It starts with a general idea of how to reach a certain objective and works out how to carry that out using available resources. In this case, the general idea was to hear from poor people in a constructive way that would help understand how best to design financing products for their benefit. A fact-finding assessment and provisional research plan were developed to enable the Chinyika community to identify the first action steps.

Following this, the ensuing evaluation will determine whether the objective has been achieved and will allow further modification as demonstrated in the following diagram.

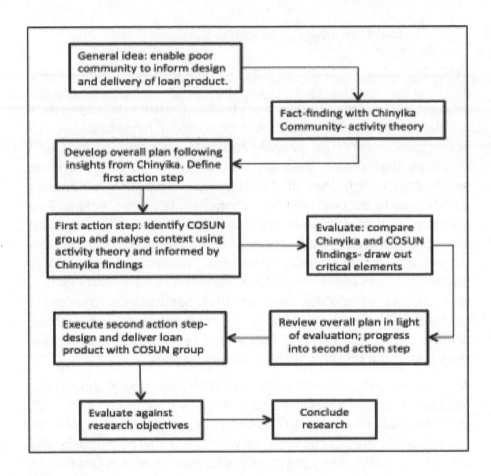

Using the Activity Theory lens, this innovative research includes an understanding of the cultural and socio-historic context that enables poor people to articulate their livelihood needs to influence microfinance services for their benefit.

Activity theory was started by the Russian Lev Vygotsky in the 1920s and aimed to understand how people bring about change in their lives through their own activities. Activity theory recognises each community as an activity system.

Both activity theory and action research work form the premise that knowledge emerges from practice, and the two approaches can be complementary.

This research was designed to respond to the following questions, as in the table below.

1a. What are poor people's voices regarding their livelihoods?
1b. How do they influence beneficial responses?
2. How can poor people's voices inform microfinance design and delivery of appropriate loan products?

ACTION	PURPOSE	QUESTIONS
Fact-finding assessment with Chinyika community using activity theory method.	Listen and learn how poor people influence beneficial actions.	1a. What are poor people's voices regarding their livelihoods?
Analysis of COSUN group using activity theory based on Chinyika community.		1b. How do they influence beneficial actions?
COSUN group informs the design of a loan and accesses it.	Create dialogue space for poor people to articulate livelihood needs and inform design of financial service.	2. How can poor people's voices inform microfinance design and delivery of appropriate loan products?

Philosophical and Theological Underpinnings of the Research

This research is concerned with how social systems are constructed and their impact on vulnerable people. It recognises that poor people are often marginalised and can experience powerlessness due to social structures that work against them.

This research also has theological leanings that recognise God's concern for the marginalised, the poor, the weak and the destitute. This concern for social justice is repeatedly echoed by the prophets and forms a special theme of Jesus' ministry. God created that which is good to benefit all people, and this aligns with the thinking that a better future must include a reformed Christian community that secures transformative solutions for the marginalised, and that listens to and responds appropriately to the voices of poor people.

My role was both as researcher and microfinance practitioner. In the interaction with the Chinyika community, I was an outsider researching their practices that led to securing food in a time of drought. In the research with COSUN, my position shifted from being an outright outsider to helping the group in designing a loan, but to a greater or lesser extent I was accepted by both communities.

The Gender Dimension

The Chinyika community is a patriarchal society and the COSUN group is an all-women group selected by a male-dominated leadership. The gender perspective recognises the challenges that women face to gain power from their own voice. Women are affected by patriarchal traditional cultures that relegate women to roles of care giving and providing for the family from meagre resources. These roles mean that women often have little time to take advantage of opportunities around them.

Women have financial needs for lifecycle events like the birth of a child, payment of school fees, rent or construction of a home. They resort to various financial mechanisms depending on the availability of disposable incomes which are often lacking, thereby denying women access to money. Women's low levels of education generally also mean a low level of financial literacy and therefore reduced opportunities to navigate the financial landscape. This research aimed to determine the extent to which women can articulate their needs to influence microfinance practitioners in positive ways.

Primary data came from direct interaction with the communities through interviews and open-ended questionnaires. Secondary data was collected from background reading about the communities under study. I was able to communicate in the local languages, and conversations were recorded and the data transcribed in the original language and then translated into English. The following is a sample:

... *ngefifine balelanda, tupelela fye umu mwine – ukukosa twalikosa, nomba wakuti tukwateko uwakututwalako pantanshi nangu ukuti uchite ichi.*	... as it has been said, we are just left behind. We are strong and we want to work, but we do not have anyone to help us develop, to tell us what to do.

In the following chapter, I will discuss the fact-finding assessment with the Chinyika community.

"Returning to our Roots"

No one was paying attention to the beautiful scenery on the drive from Harare to Tavengwa village in Gutu District of Masvingo Province, Zimbabwe. The mood in the vehicle was electric. We were excited and expectant. We had travelled from Geneva and were finally going to meet and talk to the villagers who had worked hard against all odds to achieve food security in the face of persistent drought and a runaway inflation rate following numerous economic shocks. The year was 2009. Our arrival must have been announced by the huge cloud of dust that our vehicle produced and which could be seen for miles. A crowd was waiting for us at the village, and as we alighted from the vehicle they broke into a welcome song and dance. We joined in. Soon after, we were led into a hut where the men sat on stools that had been arranged on one side of the room, and I sat on the floor with the women on the other side. The formal introductions and greetings were an elaborate ceremony that we were informed was part of the culture.

Soon after, Tendai, the leader of the village committee, took over and talked about returning to their roots in their quest for food security. She narrated in the local language, Shona, how the famine became too hard to bear and they turned to their headmen for a solution:

Vakationa tiri mukati mwenzara vakaitawo pfungwa dzekutibetsera ... vakazova nechidzidzo kutidzidzisa icho chekuti kuti nzara iyi ipere tinofanira kurima chinhu chinonzi rukweza chair-imwa navakuru vedu vakare – Vakuru vedu vakare vairima.	They [headmen] saw the hunger and decided to teach us how we could sur-vive and end the hunger. They told us about how our ancestors survived by farming sorghum. They started teach-ing us how to grow sorghum just as our ancestors did.

Tendai narrated how the persistent drought had increasingly reduced their maize yields until they had next to nothing and had to deal with hunger. Maize is the main ingredient in the staple food. The community appealed to their Headman who was then living in Harare to help them find a solution. Going back to their roots enabled them to start on the path to recovery by considering growing hardy crops like millet and sorghum that were better suited for the arid conditions.

The Background

The Chinyika community belongs to the Shona-speaking people, the largest ethnic group in Zimbabwe and Mozambique, consisting of several linguistic dialect groups like Korekore, Zezuru, Manyika, Ndau, Karanga and Kalanga. The Shona settled on the Zimbabwe plateau around 1 AD, having moved from the north across the Zambezi River. They settled on the hills, where they constructed stone houses (*dzimba dzemabwe*), and were credited with being very industrious agriculturalists, animal herders and fishermen. To supplement their livelihoods, the Shona were adept at incorporating wild plants and insects in their diet. They made good use of their harsh environments by being responsive to opportunities. The Portuguese introduced maize as a European crop in the sixteenth century, and the Shona quickly adapted to the farming of maize as an additional crop.

Though the environment was harsh for growing maize, there was a high demand by colonialists, who used it to feed their hired labourers and provided a ready market for surplus maize stocks. Thus, maize gained importance as a trading commodity that brought much-needed cash to meet payment of the various newly introduced taxes. By and by, more attention was paid to maize as the other grains were excluded from the commodity market. Those locals who went to work for the mines adapted to eating *sadza* made from maize meal in place of traditional grains. Food production became centred on growing maize. The Chinyika community is located in a region which is dry, prone to droughts and ill-suited for maize growing.

The Country Context

Colonialism destabilised the agrarian economy that had been under the control of traditional chiefs and headmen. The first white settlers, discovering that the region was not endowed in mineral resources, turned their interest to farming and acquired land rights from the indigenous people in accordance with established legal concessions. Further pieces of legislation served to separate the indigenous or native lands from those held by the settlers, who had also become the colonisers. These instruments gave legal control of land to the settlers and consequently alienated the indigenous people. Some reports indicate that indigenous people were dispossessed of over 80% of their cattle, while their lands were reassigned for mines, farms and industries. Indigenous people were moved away from their ancestral lands, and this mass movement into designated reserves created overcrowding and land degradation due to over-cultivation, leading to poor yields.

Zimbabwe was first known as Southern Rhodesia and ruled by the British South African Company under charter from Britain between 1890 and 1923. It was then annexed and continued to be ruled by the existing government as a white protectorate under the British government until 1953. At this point, it became part of the Rhodesia and Nyasaland federation, consisting of Northern Rhodesia, Southern Rhodesia and Nyasaland, now known as Zambia, Zimbabwe and Malawi. Following Ghana's independence in 1957, a wind of change resulted in Britain ending the Rhodesia and Nyasaland federation in 1963, and soon after (1964) granting independence to Northern Rhodesia and Nyasaland. Southern Rhodesia remained under the white protectorate government, which proclaimed a Unilateral Declaration of Independence (UDI) in 1965 against the wishes of the British government, who wanted independence for indigenous people.

Trade and investment sanctions from Britain and the United Nations, along with guerrilla uprising from the indigenous people, culminated in a long and protracted struggle for independence from the white-led government, which was finally won in 1979. Robert Gabriel Mugabe was elected Prime Minister and formal independence endorsed on 18th April 1980. He became President in 1987. However, the new government did not have much control over the land, the main productive asset of the country, and therefore little control over food security.

To rectify this anomaly, the government instituted a land redistribution exercise that was highly criticised and impacted negatively on commercial farming. The resultant poor agricultural performance compounded by persistent drought led to reduced food reserves and ultimately famine. Zimbabwe was criticised on other issues including political violence, restricted media and reluctance to allow EU elections monitoring for transparency. The ensuing sanctions had serious repercussions on the economy, the most telling one being the ever-increasing rate of inflation, reported at 231 million %in October 2008. Poverty became endemic, necessitating food and other aid to poor families, though this was far from adequate. Rural areas were particularly affected – with a diminishing supply of subsidised agricultural inputs, support to small farmers waned and disappeared. Poverty took root. Chinyika is one of the places which was adversely affected by this turn of events.

Analysis of the Chinyika Community as an Activity System

Traditionally, the Shona staple food was based on grain crops like millet and sorghum, as they were prolific even in harsh conditions and had multiple uses. The pounded meal was used to prepare a thick porridge called *sadza*, which is still eaten as a staple food, and for brewing beer. Celebrations to commemorate ancestral spirits could only be done with beer brewed using malt from traditional crops. Additionally, sweet sorghum reeds were chewed like sugarcane and used as a snack. The stalks were used for building, bedding, fencing, and especially for constructing granaries to store the grains. Furthermore, food production as an outcome of the activity system engendered the social norms of the community on the importance of sharing food. The proverb sums it up:

"ukama igaswa hunozadziswa nekudya" (relationships on their own are never adequate; they are only made adequate by people sharing food). Sharing food helped strengthen relationships.

Limited-quality agricultural inputs and persistent drought affected food production and ensuing famine, leading to cycles of poverty. Tendai elaborates:

Tiri mukati mwenzara ... takararama mukati mazwo tichirya chakata ...	During the time of famine ... we survived by eating wild fruits ...

Community members discussed their predicament with their Headman, who was at the time located in the city. They knew he was their point of recourse and he accepted that obligation by virtue of his position. He provided a short-term solution by sending bags of maize to the village, while working on a longer-term process. He knew that reliance on maize as a single staple crop combined with persistent drought presented a poor set of circumstances for food security. Through a research process that included his subjects, he realised that a long-term solution needed to be steeped in their historical and cultural background. Their ancestors produced crops that were more resilient to the droughts often experienced in the region.

The Chinyika community is a closely knit Shona community with traditional connections that include a common ancestry. The Shona communities consist of a kinship system of closely or remotely related persons, with precedence and succession, showing superiority and subordination without absolute equality. This means that there is always someone of authority to look up to. The structure starts with *rudzi* – a widely scattered body of people sharing the same clan or *mutupo*, consisting of several sub-clans sharing the same name or *chidawo*, specific to each separate sub-clan. As a patrilineal society, the *chidawo* passes from the natural father; thus, people can claim to belong even without actual kinship. The larger family or *mhuri* includes in-laws and uterine kinsmen.

In the hierarchical structure, there is a clear line of authority from the paramount chief through to the subjects under a village Headman. The chief (*ishe*) retains the highest authority of the tribe (*nyika* or *rudzi*). This is divided into smaller units called wards or *dunhu* (*madunhu* in plural) under the control of the Ward Headman. Each Ward has under it several villages (*musha*) under the hereditary village Headman (*samusha* or *sabuku*), and membership to this community is based on kinship and/or residence. Within the hierarchical structure, the *samusha* is the head of the principal family and controls the whole village.

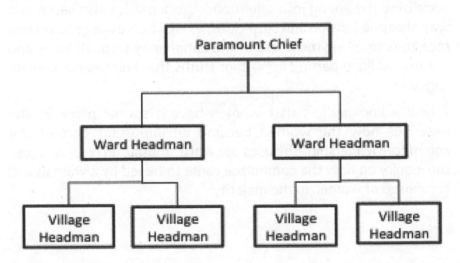

Originally, the villages consisted of six to twenty-five people with kindred connections. The rotational farming methods made it imperative for this small village unit to keep moving in pursuit of available arable land. Government policies that relegated Africans to native reserve areas meant less mobility and bigger villages, though still functioning under the established structures.

The Shona have a strong connection to the land – a shared space which people call *musha* or home. *Musha* also connotes a common location, common traditions and interests, a common way of life and common values. It denotes a strong sense of togetherness, which determines how they live as a community. They observe social values and norms that re-enforce social cohesion. The production of crops bring together the community to accomplish the labour-intensive work of land preparation, sowing, weeding, harvesting, husking and storage. Co-operative work is achieved through work parties, which call for reciprocity. The work parties are further used as a way of socialising the young into adulthood. Work parties also serve as a way of easing tension and suspicions, as well as providing corrective measures to erring members of the community through jokes and teasing, while imparting important truths that knit the community together.

Tendai acknowledges that women have a special place as she describes how the women became an important part of the committee leadership. She uses the word "*musha*" in responding to the inquiry on how the committee came to be led by a woman and composed of women in the majority:

*Vakaona kuti madzimai anogona kubata basa iri nenyaya yekuti vanamai ndivo vanochengeta **musha** kazhinji – ndovarimi vanorima varipamkova.*	They saw that women can do this work because they keep the home ... they are the farmers who are located at home.

The connection between women and the home is very fitting in the context of the Shona culture, which is patrilineal. It is the woman who organises the practical aspects of the home. Her main role is to look after her home: this is the basic meaning of *musha*.

Farming and religion were intricately intertwined. Traditional ceremonies like *mishashe* were done to appease the ancestral *mhondoro* and as thanksgiving for the harvest. These ceremonies used traditionally brewed beer from *zvio*, the traditional millet of the Shona. The religion of the Shona is purposed to keep the people on the land and close to nature. Tendai explained the place of ancestral spirits as a strong factor that binds them:

*Iyi nzvimbo ino iyi nozwamuri kuona izvi ndodzaiva **ndotsika dzedu** dzaiitwa nev-abereki vedu kare – zwatirikurarama ndozwairarama nevabereki vedu kare – saka ndozwatiri kurararamao nazwo. Nozwamurikuona izvi ndizvo zwaiitikwa nevabereki vedu kare.*	This place and all you see represent our **traditions** – what our ancestors did – how we are staying alive now is the same way our ancestors stayed alive. What you see us doing now is what our ancestors did.

When she says *ndotsika dzedu* (our traditions), she is implying a strong connection to a common ancestry. The phrase "*tsika dzedu*" talks of their values, customs, norms and traditions.

The voices of the community became an important factor in the activity system. The villages raise their voices with their Headman about the need to find a solution against hunger. The village Headman had authority over his village to bring about benevolent actions. He was also competent to realise the need for new knowledge when problems arose.

At the direction of the Headman, the community set up a village committee to refocus the community from maize to millet. They distributed millet seed to the villagers and provided access to government agricultural extension services for support for modern farming methods. The committee dealt with the obstacles through community participation in activities along with incentives. The learning process included field days where practical demonstrations were held.

Summary of the Analysis

With this analysis the following research questions were addressed:

1a. What are poor people's voices regarding their livelihoods?
1b. How do they influence beneficial actions?

The strong community structure of the Shona people provides a dependable support system. Consequently, when famine strikes, the voices of the poor are activated, but in their desperation and lack of a solution, they resort to foraging the forest for wild vegetation, realising that the problem was beyond their experience and knowledge to resolve.

The community structure allows the poor recourse through the Headman, depositing their individual and collective voices in him. The Headman realises that the community does not have the capacity to address the food problem in the face of persistent drought. Through specific research, he comes up with a long-term solution. In this way, he enables the voices of the community to influence processes that benefit them. The Headman is a critical figure who assumes the collective voice of the community and attempts to craft a solution for the rest of the community. He takes on his role in a benevolent way and becomes the champion of the community. He has the authority, respect and recognition to do so.

In the following chapter, we will review the COSUN group in peri-urban Zambia to provide a basis for comparison with the Chinyika community in terms of what the voices of poor people are and how they inform processes that benefit them.

Comparing the COSUN Women
and the Chinyika Women

In the first chapter, we encountered Jenala and some of the women in the COSUN group. Having picked up some aspects that contributed to the Chinyika story in Chapter Three I will draw out parameters for comparing the two communities to generate an analytical framework. The comparison aims to respond to the research questions:

1a. What are poor people's voices about their livelihoods?
1b. How do those voices influence actions that contribute to their livelihood needs?

Zambia Country Context

Like the history of Zimbabwe, Zambia was under the jurisdiction of the British South African Company, a mining prospecting company in former Northern Rhodesia and Katanga (now Zambia and Congo). To ferry copper to South Africa, they built a railway line along which cities and towns were established and which created a demand for labour. Able-bodied men in rural areas moved to the mines and cities for paid labour. As discussed in the first chapter, various pieces of legislature progressively allowed miners to stay in the cities at the expiry of their work contracts, and to bring their families from their villages. Squatter settlements ensued from this rural-to-urban migration. The COSUN group are in one of the squatter settlements.

Activity System Comparison

Both the Chinyika and COSUN communities are faced with precarious livelihoods without a solution or expert knowledge to find solutions. This raises questions as to the usefulness of un-enlightened agency in bringing about transformation. The Chinyika activity system has a farming history that has inherent benefits: food security, social cohesion, utility value and as a connector to their religion and common ancestry. When famine strikes, they address this problem through an established channel – their Headman. The COSUN women, on the other hand, come from different ethnic groups and are in the urban settlement because of migration. They need cash to support their livelihoods. They depend on external support. Their problems happen at various levels:

- Some of the COSUN women are widows and others have husbands who have lost their jobs. Without assured income, they need to find another way of earning money. They have no solution to that.
- They participate in manual labour but feel cheated as they do not get what they expected. Their leaders let them down.
- The COSUN women have no way of getting capital to sustain their businesses.
- CPSCC feel that the NGO left without a sustainable strategy for the continuity of the programme.

The community has no place of recourse to deal with these problems.

Functional Structure

The Chinyika activity system has a supportive structure for community members. The system engenders togetherness and members have a common heritage. When there is a problem, community members know where to present that problem – they have a community dialogue space.

The COSUN women, on the other hand, come from different ethnic groups and belong to a group whose formation was facilitated by an external party. As an affiliate of CPSCC, they are beholden to that leadership. They need benevolent leaders to help them out of their poverty. The structure does not serve the COSUN women – they lack dialogue space.

Ability to Identify Problems

Critical to food production, the Chinyika community use their knowledge as agriculturalists; they can till the land and plant their crop. The persistent drought and subsequent famine highlighted an inherent problem within the activity system for which a solution was needed. It also raised an issue about the capacity of the community to recognise the limitations of their knowledge and devise a solution in a timely manner. The critical role of leadership, especially through the Headman, led to expansive learning because of new information in the community to resolve the food security problem.

The COSUN activity system is predicated on the members utilising capital and skills to engage in economic activities that would earn them an income. They find themselves lacking on both counts, without anyone to help them. The COSUN group seem to have their doubts about the usefulness of CPSCC as a complementing activity system, but still look up to them for leadership.

The Chinyika community had a competent Headman who could undertake actions for the benefit of the community. Reverting to grain crops made a direct connection with the way their ancestors lived. The community was able to start on a journey of sense-making as they reconnected with their roots.

The dynamics of the COSUN group are steeped in the programming left by PROSPECT. The CPSCC leaders do not seem to have the specific interest of the COSUN group as their priority. The women recall how the unfair treatment started during the food-for-work programme when they were promised free water and jobs at water points, but this did not happen. They feel cheated and taken advantage of – the dialogue space is inhibiting.

Research Questions: Voices Influencing Livelihood Actions

In the two cases, the communities knew when they were in trouble. In Chinyika's case, the desperation and hopelessness of their situation created the right space for them to act. Their voices were heard and the Headman had unquestionable authority to act on behalf of his people for their good, which he did. He was benevolent and provided pathways to sustainable solutions with an added benefit of expanding learning for the community. Thus, the existing dialogue space revealed the underlying problem and influenced action towards a sustainable solution.

The pre-COSUN story is that of desperation. Despite the leadership training, benevolent behaviours did not take root with the local leaders: the story is disjointed. The COSUN women's story does not lead to a transformative outcome. Their voices do not have the capacity to influence long-term livelihood outcomes.

Chinyika Community Critical Incident Towards Action

For the Chinyika activity system, drought was a predictable event in that region. The area was arid and the community had already experienced several spells of drought. The question arises as to why the Chinyika community did not take corrective measures way before the 2004 drought. The community had an effective dialogue space. Until this point, the community had managed to produce enough to survive on, albeit in reducing quantities. The drought of 2004 pushed the community to the very end of their resources. Their quest for survival made them resort to foraging the forest for wild fruits; socialising around food stopped as there was no food to share; some people simply waited to die unless they received relief food from CARE International and from their Headman.

The extreme behaviours caused by the desperation became the critical incident, sudden and overwhelming, requiring a survival strategy. The Chinyika community remember in detail how the famine affected relationships and how they had to resort to wild fruits. They recall how the food aid was less than adequate to meet their dietary needs and recall desperate measures they took, including calling on their Headman to send relief food.

Furthermore, the critical incident occurred at the time that the Headman also realised that he would be the next in line for chieftain. The famine presented the opportunity for him to cement that position. He redefined the problem and located it in the fact that the region was arid and would not easily grow maize. As a person of influence, he assumed the role of representing the collective agency of the community to bring about a new learning. The role of the Headman was critical in coming up with a solution. The community regarded him as an authentic representation of their needs, and he was therefore able to engage proactively with another system and influence the community towards a solution. His was a strong community voice that echoed the voices of his subjects.

COSUN Community – Challenges of Urban Development

The COSUN situation was different. The context in the squatter settlement is that of enforced norms. With different ethnic backgrounds, areas of commonality were almost non-existent and donors wanting to work in these communities had to start with nurturing the groups and building local leadership. However, experience revealed that benevolent behaviours could not be assumed as training outcomes. The COSUN women believe that their leaders took advantage of the situation and siphoned resources meant for the bigger community. Jenala has this to say:

Baleikata sana mumenso – makamaka abakuntanshi. Balebula filya ifintu baleshitisha, balekwatilamo indalama ... abengi balikula ifintu ifingi sana ukupitila muli ifi.	The leaders duped the people. They sold the foodstuff and pocketed the money ... a lot of them build structures [e.g. houses] out of this.

In the Chinyika case, the Headman's motive was to ensure long-term sustainability of food security. His understanding of the problem included his recollection of the versatility of grain crops against maize. At a social level, he understood that he would need the support of the other chiefs in convincing the community of the need to change focus from maize to grain crops. He also understood that they needed a new way of knowing through a learning process. At a personal level, his actions were driven by his motive as future paramount chief. He saw the need to align his personal motives for the throne with the needs of the community. Furthermore, a proposition that recognised the importance of going back to grain crops made him enjoin traditional with modern agricultural practices, an action that would endear him to the community. This alignment made it possible to move the community towards a sustainable solution.

The COSUN case has several motives that may not have aligned. PROSPECT was set up to pilot a community-driven development approach whose success would have informed replications across CARE International's structure and other development agencies. While PROSPECT's move to provide water as an object motive could have aligned with that of the COSUN women, the reality of using local leaders to take over the running of CPSCC created a discordant fit. The leaders who were trained by PROSPECT responded to

PROSPECT's project design expectation for local leadership. There is no evidence that these are people whose motive was to ensure poverty reduction for the community. The COSUN women's experiences with CPSCC suggest a motive that was misaligned and therefore a failure to inform sustainable solutions.

Other motives were at play at the time of the PROSPECT project. Several donors had embraced the sustainable livelihoods approach that espoused holistic and people-centred development riding on community strengths for sustainability. CARE International had similarly embraced the Households Livelihoods Framework. It can be argued, therefore, that one of the motives was to try out this bottom-up approach. A different motive could be linked to the fact that CARE International had around the same time started a microfinance institution in Lusaka and that may have inspired the community-driven microfinance in PROSPECT. This congregation of motives may have excluded motive alignments with the most vulnerable and thus caused the frustrations that the women experienced.

Informing the Theoretical Framework

The analysis identified five key elements that seem essential for the voices of poor people to influence their livelihoods and to inform interventions that facilitate livelihood support. These are: the context, the structure, the object motive, the ability to identify the problem and the action trigger.

The Context

The Chinyika community had a hierarchical authority that ensured all members of the community had a voice. The COSUN group did not have this benefit. It is therefore necessary for the community to have a context that facilitates individual and collective agency to articulate their needs.

The Structure

In the Chinyika case, the structure permitted recourse – they could go to their Headman. The COSUN structure, on the other hand, did not enable such interactions. The structure should therefore enable community members to know how to handle vexing situations and who to go to, and to provide a dependable point of recourse.

The Object-Motive Alignment

The Chinyika case reflects an easier process towards object-motive alignment because the Headman was part of the community and had legitimate responsibility over the welfare of the community. He also had an added object motive as in-coming chief. In the COSUN case, a consortium that included the government, donors and CARE International externally engineered the developmental agenda. The object motives were disparate. There is therefore a need for parties driving a development agenda to ensure adequate alignment of motives for development solutions that are commonly owned.

Ability to Identify Problems

In the Chinyika case, the community reacted to the famine they felt in the immediate present. However, the Headman realised a deep-rooted problem that required a more sustainable solution. The COSUN group did not have this advantage. The capability of individual and collective agency is greatly assisted by the inherent competence of those intending to exercise such agency. There is therefore a need to identify the underlying problems to come up with appropriate solutions that last.

The Action Trigger

People can adapt to their environments and normalise problematic situations until a specific event triggers action. In the Chinyika case, it was the critical incident of foraging for wild vegetation that triggered action. The COSUN case, on the other hand, was in a situation of decreased incomes that had been protracted and may have become normative. This is evidenced by the fact that the community has leaders, but members continue looking for benevolent leaders. This raises the question of what happens when there is no obvious action trigger. There must be a way of defining the acceptable standard before livelihoods deteriorate. This again points to strong and benevolent leadership that would determine certain livelihood standards, below which action would need to be taken.

Analytical Framework from Case Studies

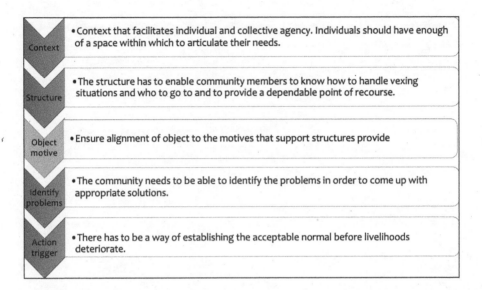

Context
- Context that facilitates individual and collective agency. Individuals should have enough of a space within which to articulate their needs.

Structure
- The structure has to enable community members to know how to handle vexing situations and who to go to and to provide a dependable point of recourse.

Object motive
- Ensure alignment of object to the motives that support structures provide

Identify problems
- The community needs to be able to identify the problems in order to come up with appropriate solutions.

Action trigger
- There has to be a way of establishing the acceptable normal before livelihoods deteriorate.

The framework developed using the cultural-historical activity system lens highlights the complexities of communities, which cannot be ignored when evaluating the capacity of poor people's voices to inform development interventions that benefit them.

The following chapters will focus on the COSUN members using the dialogue space provided by the research to articulate their livelihood needs and design a loan product that responds to those needs. They proceed to access the loan they design and provide some input on the experience.

COSUN Women Informing a Loan Process

"Vimozi navimozi monga sitiziba vimene vichitika" (same old stuff – as if we do not know what happens), Pelile mumbles in Nyanja. She is visibly upset and continues:

Ine niona kuti paja poyamba tinayambila iyi nkhani ninaona kuti chabwera chintu chachilendo kapena chakuti tingapezerepo thandizo tonse – lomba nionanso kuti nkhani ilikuchinja kuti ibwererenso kumanja kwacooperative kwamene tinalephera kale – ndiye mwamene naonela.	I see that when we started [the research] it looked like something new that would help all of us – now I can see things changing – going back to the cooperative where we failed before – this is what I am seeing.

This is happening in our weekly meeting. Today, 26th June 2012, is an important day. This is the day when we are discussing the loan that the women were eagerly awaiting – they are all present. This is the space where the women would define the structure and process to obtain a loan that would meet their needs. The discussions will contribute to answering the research question:

However, the previous day, the leaders of CPSCC, who provide oversight to the COSUN group, had invited me for a meeting to discuss some issues around the loans that were part of the research. This was surprising because I had not yet discussed the loan process with the women. They obviously had been following our meetings. This was gratifying. They assured me that they trusted the women to make good decisions and to pay back as expected. This was all good news to me. However, they had some requirements that were new to me and they wanted me to consider them and comply. These are:

- They wanted the women to continue paying into their savings accounts with CPSCC.
- They wanted to monitor the loans that the research process would provide. The loans would therefore have to be disbursed through them.
- They wanted to hold a three-day workshop with the women to discuss how all this would work.
- They wanted to sign a contract with me to incorporate the above aspects and to agree on the commission they would earn for doing the work. Ultimately, this was not done.
- Finally, they wanted me to include some women who, they said, were part of the COSUN group but had been left out of the initial meetings.

In my response, I mentioned that the workshop was not part of the research process, but that I would inform the COSUN women who would then make a decision on the way forward regarding all the matters they had tabled with me. I presented these to the women the following day, and this is what Pelile had an issue with.

The Women Discuss the Request from their Leaders

During the meeting, I informed the women regarding the request from their leaders. It then transpired that some of them had been invited to a side meeting with the leaders a few days earlier. It was clear that not all the women were at this meeting. Chinyanta was there and she narrates:

... ija day banakamba kuti chamene tangenelamo ise aba pamanyumba pathu sibazibapo sibakaya kuno but ba cooperative bonse pamanyumba bazivapo – chipepukako kuti ngati ni day yoika ndalama olo mabusiness yathu, vazivapo mumanyumba mwathu bazayambochita monga day imozi bapitamo kuona mwamene tichitila mabusiness yathu that's why banakamba kuti bangenemo bamene baziba mabusiness chifukwa aba sibazabwera mumanyumba mwathu – bazayamba chabe kubwera pacooperative.	... that day when we met, they [the leaders] told us the reason they had decided to get involved in the process is that [the researcher] she does not know our homes, she does not know this area but the leaders know all our homes. On the repayment date, they would make it easy for us by monitoring us and making sure our businesses are running well.

It was apparent from these conversations that the leaders had managed to convince the women present of the need for the CPSCC leaders' support. The women agreed to complete the CPSCC loan application forms and to continue saving, but they were not too happy with the fact that their leaders wanted to disburse the loans, hold a workshop and monitor them. Pelile's views were representative of most of the women.

I was more concerned about the implications of this development: would the women give up their voice and submit to the desires of their leaders? Even after much deliberation among themselves, there was no solution coming forth. Some of the women felt the need to give in to their leaders while others were visibly reluctant to do so. The choice they had was to either give in to their leaders or stand up to them and make their own decisions. I sensed that, if they took the latter stance, it would be seen as an affront and something unusual. I could also see that the opportunity that the research had given to the women to speak and say what they wanted was slipping – it would be difficult to be assertive in the face of the demands from their leaders. We made some agreements as follows:

Workshop

The women did not see the need for a workshop. Rather, they explained that in the past such workshops were occasions for eating.

Mthunzi: Awe ... imwe mufunika kuti mubamasulule kuti ngati bacooperative bafuna workshop ndiye kuti kumafunika vakudya aba [vacooperative] sibangakonze vakudya – bazafunika kukonza vakudya nivamadam. Bophunzitsa nabo bazafunika kulipiliwa – sitiziba kuti babalipila zingati. So ife kuno tikavomela kuti kufunika workshop, so imwe lomba ni bill yanu. Izankhala kuli imwe bill yokonza workshop. –	Mthunzi: No ... you need to explain to her [researcher] that if the cooperative leaders want a workshop, there will be need for food and the cooperative leaders do not provide. She will have to prepare all that, including payment to the workshop facilitators – we do not know how much they are paid. So if we agree that we want a workshop, it will be your bill.

This was new information for me and I had no way of verifying it without going back to the same leaders who were bringing new requirements. I reminded the women that my role was to engage with them in designing a loan that would benefit them and that all the meetings we had had so far were adequate without the need for a workshop. I re-emphasised that the whole project was about listening and responding to their voices and that the leaders consented to that at the beginning of the process. The decision of the way forward lay with them. The women explained their discontent with the workshops:

Chinyanta: ... tankhala namaworkshop yambili tilinamabuku yambili – mukafuna tingabwele nayo yonse yo entrepreneurship tili nayo. Pelile: Ninali nakamba poyamba paja kuti ivi mwamene yapita nkhani niiona kuti yazinguluka futi ibwerera futi kucooperative. Sonaya: Emo balila that's why tenzokamba kuti bamatidyakilila. Ndiye cholinga chaworkshop ... [Voices and laughter] Heavy tea nefyakulilapo elo lunch ubwali nenkoko nangu inama balaleta elyo indalama mukafumya eikulu. Mthunzi: Aya ma workshop naife vophunzira tifunika kudyesewa. Timadyesewa zoona – nkuku na nyama, na drink namanzi.	Chinyanta: ... we have already had many workshops – we have the books to show for it. We can bring the books to show you – entrepreneurship is there as well. Pelile: I had said when we started that the way this matter was being handled would take us back to the cooperative. Sonaya: That is how they benefit – that is why we said that they take advantage of us. That is the goal of the workshop ... heavy tea with food then ubwali [staple dish] with chicken or beef – the money you will be required to pay is much. Mthunzi: In these workshops, even us being taught need to be fed – and we do get fed – chicken and beef, with drinks and water.

The women finally agreed to proceed without the support of CPSCC or having the workshop. They felt that they could monitor themselves.

Addition of new members

The women felt that it was rather late in the process to bring in new members. They felt that the new members would not have the advantage of the discussions that had led to the loan being designed in a particular way and that there could be a discordant relationship if the new people joined.

Following these decisions, the leaders expressed their disappointment for being left out. They also claimed that the women had selected new leaders without permission when other leaders were already there. This was an interesting and surprising turn of events. This group was chosen by these same leaders to participate in the research. If there were already leaders in this group, why did they leave them out of the research? They now looked at my research with some suspicion but allowed us to continue.

The Women Design the Loans

The women designed the loan product focused on the following parameters:

Loan amount

The women agreed that each member should ask only for money they would be able to pay back. Each member qualified for the amount they asked for. This was very different from the process used by CPSCC, where loans were pegged to the amount of savings that everyone had made.

My reflections

Standard practice is that the purpose of the loan determines the conditions. An enterprise loan would be structured according to the business cash flows, whereas a housing loan would be attached to the incomes that would be servicing the loan. Part of the intent of the study was to enable women to structure the loan to meet their financial needs in relation to an economic activity that microfinance institutions would typically fund. The capacity to pay is an important element for the women; however, it did not justify the debt. The conditions the women stipulated were driven by their various household needs and dissatisfaction with conditions of previous loans, even where they did not have a good understanding of the rationale for those conditions. Risky as the loans may have been, money was a rare commodity, and the women sought to use the opportunity to obtain as much as they would be able to pay back without attracting penalties.

Group guarantee

The women agreed to work on the basis of trust and not use the group guarantee approach that would pull the full loan amount and require the group to guarantee the full amount.

My reflections

This would not be permissible if a microfinance institution was granting the loan. The absence of tangible collateral required that the group agree on collective responsibility for individual loans.

The repayment period

The CPSCC requirements were that loans be repaid over a six-month period. The women decided on a nine-month period with monthly instalment payments on the 10th of the following month.

My reflections

It was not clear why the women needed to do the repayments on the 10th of each following month. Several women used the money to extend and/or repair their houses so they could put in tenants. I can only imagine these women repaid their loans from rental income after the end of each month. That was their regular and assured source of money. I also wondered if some of their merchandise was sold on credit and payment only received at the end of the month. Weekly meetings stopped after they got the loans, so I was unable to verify.

Grace period

The loans given by CPSCC required that instalment repayments start in the following month. This did not sit well with the women, and they varied this condition by including a one-month grace period.

My reflections

The change in the repayment period and the need for a grace period seemed to align more with the fact that the women had been dissatisfied with the six-month repayment period and lack of grace period expected by CPSCC. There was no other reason connected to their businesses.

Penalty clause on delayed payments

CPSCC required them to pay a penalty for delayed instalments. The women removed the penalty clause completely because they felt that it impacted negatively on their profits.

My reflections

This looked like another reaction to the negative experiences that the women wanted to avoid. Given the weak business propositions and the pressure to eke out a living using borrowed money, it is easy to see how such a penalty could be seen as eroding profits rather than enforcing discipline against defaulting.

Peer support

To provide one another with peer support, they agreed to visit each other and consult on their businesses. This is something that they would not have done previously, as each one fended for themselves. The women also agreed that they would continue meeting every Wednesday to discuss progress on their businesses and loan repayments. This was in line with research expectations, as agreed upon at the outset.

Interest calculation

The women understood that they needed to pay interest on the loan, but had no idea how that was arrived at. They had little understanding of how interest is worked out generally and how the cooperative arrived at what they charged on the loans they issued. The calculations were complex and beyond their capacity to comprehend. They were also confusing the interest they received on their savings of 10% per year. It appeared that the whole concept of interest was too technical for them, and explanations served to only confuse them further. This is an area in which they would not inform the financial arrangement owing to their lack of technical knowhow.

The Women Stop Meeting

At the beginning of the research process, we agreed on weekly meetings. Attendance was good before the loans were given out. Afterwards, numbers dwindled till we officially stopped.

After they got the money, the dynamics changed. The women got busy and threw out their own rules. It was clear to me that the women needed the money to do their businesses. In retrospect, I realised that the possibility of getting the loan may have motivated them to faithfully attend meetings. After they got the loan, priorities changed, and there was no one to hold them accountable to their earlier commitments. They needed to use that money and ensure that by the time a repayment instalment was due, they would have money to pay in. That became the new priority. They disregarded the commitments they had made before they got the loan including meeting to reflect on their experiences using the loan. Most importantly, their action to stop meetings served to close the dialogue space that the research had opened, thereby raising the question of the women's perceptions of the usefulness of that space.

Interestingly, the women paid towards their obligations faithfully. A few delayed but came through to pay their indebtedness in full.

I was concerned about the research process – I needed their voices to inform the microfinance practice. Then I realised: this was the feedback. The women's reality of needing money to support their various activities was the motive for their initial commitment to meetings before they got the loan. This was an opportunity they were going to use. Their universe consisted of taking opportunities that are presented to them, utilising them as faithfully as they could and moving on to the next thing. My own thoughts about listening to them and learning together to come up with a sustainable solution had to be framed differently.

In the following chapter, I will review these findings in light of the analytical framework produced in Chapter Four.

A Summary of Research Findings

In this research I aimed to create a dialogue space that would enable poor people to inform the design and delivery of microfinance services that are fit for purpose. In this chapter, I will:

- assess the usefulness of the research dialogue space to the COSUN group, using the analytical framework developed in Chapter 4;
- assess the usefulness of the research dialogue space for microfinance institutions;
- assess the extent to which COSUN group members would have informed microfinance practitioners as they designed a loan product;
- enumerate issues emanating from the research dialogue space;
- articulate a theory of microfinance dialogue space using activity theory.

A Context that Encourages Voice

The women discussed their individual concerns and collectively identified common positions. Thus, the context encouraged them to express themselves and, in the process, question certain activities they did not understand. However, the dialogue space was temporary and externally driven. It was tested when the CPSCC leaders called for and had a side meeting with group members. The leaders used their power to call for the meeting and, through that, attempted to get involved in the research process. There is therefore a critical challenge in creating temporary dialogue spaces by external parties that can be overridden by the elite in the community. This would be a factor is deciding whether microfinance institutions can on their own create dialogue space for obtaining feedback from their poor clients. The strength of the Chinyika case study context lay in the fact that the dialogue space was embedded within the community.

Supportive Structure for Recourse

The structure that enabled the research, by intent, also enabled the women to inform the loan process. The women took control of the situation and were able to stand up to their leaders when they needed to. This was not easy for them given that they were effectively under the supervision of these same leaders and would have to inevitably work with them again. As discussed above, the structure provided by the research was a temporary one that would not have far-reaching benefits for the women. The structure needed to be internal to the community; owned and respect by all members of the community regardless of their economic station. The structure would also allow recourse and clear authority lines like those in the Chinyika community.

Because the research was structured to give the women a voice that would influence a process for their benefit, at the beginning the object motive seemed to be perfectly aligned between the researcher, the women and the CPSCC leaders. However, the mis-alignment became evident as the research process progressed. The CPSCC leaders' objective motive became more defined once they realised that the women would access loans: they wanted to handle the money and even earn a commission without due regard to the voices of the women. Though there was resolution to this situation, the leaders withdrew their support, which might have informed a more progressive way forward when the women decided to stop meeting. The women's object motive also became clear after they got the loan. They stopped meeting contrary to what had been agreed on at the start of the research. Without the possibility of sustained dialogue with the women, the research process concluded. Thus, a mis-alignment of the object motive was the primary reason for the conclusion of the research, underscoring the need for proper alignment of object motives in order to achieve agreed objectives. This mis-alignment of object motives was not evident at the beginning of the research and therefore raises questions about the efficacy of interventions that are externally engineered, even when preceded by needs assessments. A useful approach would be to locate the burden of aligning object motives within the community, as in the Chinyika case study.

The issue of identifying a problem in this study was overridden by the specific expectations of the study: for the women to articulate their financial needs and design a corresponding loan product. However, designing the loan product assumed that the women had a sense of their real livelihood problems that the loan would resolve. Allowing the women to design and obtain a loan assumed that they were economically active, and that it was a loan they needed. This assumption is questionable given that some COSUN members confirmed needing skills to do business. The premise of microfinance is that entrepreneurs in the informal sector often lack access to credit to grow their businesses. It is also true that poor people need money to support their livelihoods, especially in urban locations. Separating the two is important. However, a business loan represents money to be used for that specific purpose because it must be paid back from the incremental value of the business.

The question therefore arises whether microfinance practitioners should concern themselves with how the money they lend is used, and, if so, where the responsibility lies to separate money to be used in a business and money for consumption purposes. Ordinarily this separation would be done by the borrower, though interactions with the COSUN group suggest that money in their possession could be used for any pressing purpose. Community structures might be able to address this problem, if it is recognised as a problem. If not addressed, this has the potential of leading borrowers into over-indebtedness as they fail to service their loans, and consequently worsen their economic status. The structured nature of microfinance institutions leaves little opportunity to engage closely with their poor clients to tailor services that specifically respond to their needs and that are within the capacity of the microfinance institution to deliver.

Action Trigger: Establishing an Acceptable Normal

The research purposed to focus on a loan product as the action trigger. Group members endorsed this, in that some of them admitted needing money to expand their businesses and others wanted to resuscitate failed businesses if they got the money. Others complained of small amounts of money that they got from CPSCC. These utterances suggested that the women would have wanted the loans much earlier than at the time of this research. This situation is no different from the one that the Chinyika community found themselves in, where the prospects of food security kept dwindling due to successive drought. As long as the people were surviving, there was no real impetus to find a lasting solution till the drought that made them forage for wild fruits – something that was not normal to their livelihoods. Since the need for financial services is connected to livelihood needs, communities would need to consider setting acceptable living standards and identifying critical facilitative activities, like the work of microfinance institutions, that would address deviant livelihoods.

Efficacy of Research Dialogue Space

To an extent, the research dialogue space was effective. The COSUN group was able to design and access a loan that responded to their needs. The structure empowered them to stand up to their leaders. though some of them were initially going to acquiesce. However, the object motive was highly mis-aligned and led directly to the conclusion of the research. Though the women articulated their problems, the dialogue cannot be said to have engaged them to understand the underlying livelihood problems in such a way as to determine what type of financial service would be appropriate. Offering them the chance to design a loan product rode on the assumption that what they needed was a loan, and could very well have been a wrong assumption, especially given that this group was making savings without anyone recounting to them how secure it was, and how an accumulation of savings could be used in place of a loan. The research itself was the action trigger for the loan. The dialogue space did not establish livelihood standards below which facilitative action would be imperative. Thus, while the research dialogue space was somewhat useful, gaps were evident.

Usefulness of Research Dialogue Space for Microfinance

Microfinance products and services are catalytic and therefore subject to defined uses that would improve or in some cases work against livelihoods. Financial services can provide safe storage for savings, enable access to credit for business efforts, home improvement or consumption, and offer other financial-related services. In articulating their livelihood needs using the research dialogue space, the COSUN women talked about such things as their inability to take children to school, provide food and shelter and meet other social needs. They even talked about not having adequate skills to run a business. Those needs in themselves require a different response that might then benefit from using financial services. For example, a poor person wanting to pay school fees might desire a safe place to keep and accumulate several small amounts over a period to meet the required amount. Microfinance would respond by providing that safe place to keep the money until it is needed. By so doing, they enable the poor person to meet their need. Microfinance institutions can only respond with the financial services they offer to financial needs. Therefore, the extent to which these services are matched to articulated financial needs is what will determine the type and depth of impact on poor people. The following diagram demonstrates the first line of interaction where microfinance engages with communities:

Microfinance Interacting with Communities

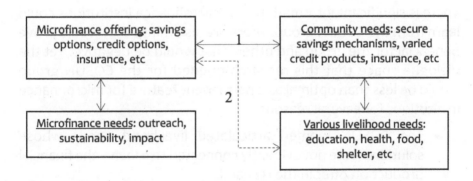

The interaction between microfinance institutions and communities represented by 1 above is the first and only line of interaction with the community. Determining livelihood impact would require understanding how a financial service is used and therefore what is happening at the second line, where microfinance institutions do not interact with the community: the dotted line 2 above represents this. The research dialogue space produced information from the COSUN women that should come out of the second line of engagement where MFIs would not operate. Dialogue spaces between the community and microfinance are limited to the first line of interaction with the community. This is likely where gaps are created in attributing impact to microfinance services. This disparity needs to be addressed in the theory of microfinance dialogue space.

However, it is important to assess how the interaction with the COSUN group in this research would have influenced microfinance.

Capturing Lessons from the COSUN Group

There is significant information that microfinance institutions could learn from the COSUN group. There are also things that would prove beneficial for the group and others that would be negative. Yet the dialogue space that this research opened for the COSUN group would be less than optimal as a permanent feature for microfinance institutions for several reasons:

- The COSUN women articulated livelihood needs whose solutions were not evidently connected to a loan – the financial product on offer in the research.
- The research assumed that all the group members had financial needs that would be met through a loan. There was no opportunity created to communicate other financial products that may have constituted an appropriate response.
- There was already an expectation for a loan in the group,

especially as they were related to CPSCC, a savings and credit cooperative.

- Microfinance institutions would not be able to invest the time and effort that this research took to understand the needs of this group.

A more useful dialogue space for microfinance institutions should enable interaction with target communities to bring out financial needs for appropriate responses.

Possible Effects of Issues Emanating from the Dialogue Space

The temporariness of this dialogue space opens possibilities for elite capture during the life of the dialogue space and possibly thereafter. The lack of community support is a result of little or no community ownership of the process. This would be inimical to any positive outcomes. It also implies the absence of community leadership with capacity to galvanise social capital for the common good. In such cases, it is the weak who will suffer, and especially women, as in the COSUN group case. The need for clear object-motive alignment is connected to ensuring acceptable living standards below which remedial action would be triggered. Without strong community structures, this responsibility would go begging. For example, the community should be able to help mitigate microfinance risks that escalate the cost of funds to poor people, or at the very least influence practitioners to provide affordable services. It would be necessary to have within the community enough competence to engage microfinance practitioners as equal interlocutors to enable responding to poor people's voices with appropriate financial products and services. The essence of robust community structures would be to ensure agentive representations in relationships with microfinance institutions, where the need for appropriate responses will be cardinal given the financial complexities that may be beyond the understanding of most recipients of these services, living in poverty.

This participatory action research introduced an innovation that recommends microfinance practitioners to consider using activity theory as a lens with which to conduct holistic assessments of communities that microfinance targets. We will consider that as we develop a theory of microfinance dialogue space in the following discussion.

Towards a Theory of Microfinance Dialogue Space

The research questions had two phases: the first one to understand the efficacy of poor people's voices; and the second one to enable poor people to inform the design of a loan. The first phase developed an analytical framework which identified the need for a community dialogue space along with critical elements needed to enable poor people's voices to influence actions that benefit them. The success that the Chinyika community experienced in securing food to counter the famine was because of the effectiveness of that community dialogue space. In the second phase, the COSUN group were afforded dialogue space to inform the design of a loan that they later accessed. In assessing the efficacy of this dialogue space, this research identified the value and limitations for both the communities involved and the microfinance institutions.

Livelihood discussions that would take place in the community dialogue space would to a large extent be removed from direct interaction with microfinance institutions, but could be impacted by financial services as long as they are successfully matched. Thus, the research identifies a microfinance dialogue space separate from the community dialogue space, where financial services can respond to identified financial needs and in so doing, respond to the voices of poor people.

A microfinance institution represents an operational system providing financial services to targeted communities. To achieve this goal, the institution undertakes several activities to ensure the desired outcomes of appropriate outreach and organisational sustainability. The positive impact on client's lives is a desired outcome but can only be achieved with community engagement. Similarly, a community in poverty would need to generate an understanding of livelihood needs that can use financial services as a solution. They would then want to enjoin a microfinance institution to access these services. Utilising these financial services would lead to social outcomes like moving people out of poverty, making sure people accumulate enough of their own funds for eventualities, or to support money management efforts. Thus, the participatory action research has identified two dialogue spaces that can be represented in the diagram overleaf.

The Community and Microfinance Dialogue Spaces

The dialogue space created within the community is the place where poor people can articulate their needs. The microfinance dialogue space is where microfinance practitioners can interact with

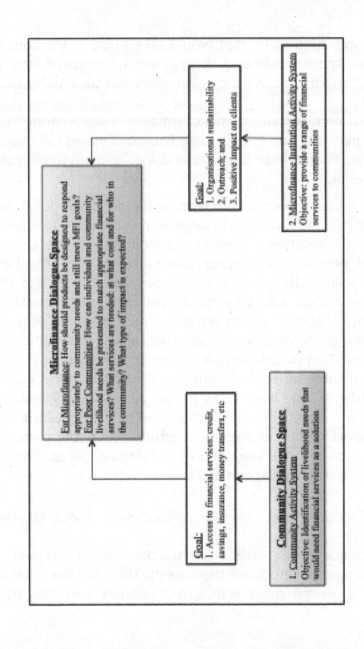

Microfinance Institution Activity System
Objective: provide a range of financial services to communities

Goal:
1. Organisational sustainability
2. Outreach; and
3. Positive impact on clients

Microfinance Dialogue Space

For Microfinance: How should products be designed to respond appropriately to community needs and still meet MFI goals?

For Poor Communities: How can individual and community livelihood needs be matched to appropriate financial services? What services are needed at what cost and for who in the community? What type of impact is expected?

Goal:
1. Access to financial services: credit, savings, insurance, money transfers, etc

Community Dialogue Space

Community Activity System
Objective: Identification of livelihood needs that would need financial services as a solution

community structures to meet their own objectives of sustainability, outreach and impact while responding to community financial needs. The need for transformative impacts forms the area of overlap that enables successful transactions. The efficacy of this space will depend on the efficacy of the community dialogue space in matching livelihood needs to financial services. In developing a theory for dialogue space, therefore, it would be useful to consider a microfinance institution as an activity system interacting with the community, which is also an activity system.

A Theory of Dialogue Space for Microfinance

Microfinance institutions (MFIs) can generate new ways of listening by intentionally seeking to understand the dynamics within the community. This expectation could be incorporated in feasibility studies that MFIs conduct as they enter into a community. Communities also could position themselves to interact with MFIs in the MFI dialogue space as equal interlocutory partners. The theory of MFI dialogue space would ensure the following characteristics:

Leadership

Community leaders to provide an understanding of the structure of the community so as to locate microfinance services. This level of inquiry would also aim to find out what dialogue spaces exist in the community and how they function. The idea would be to ascertain how social capital is galvanised and how benefits pass on to community members. It would also help demonstrate the existence of altruism within the leadership.

Structure

The structure would demonstrate points of discourse and recourse for the community. These would become useful for the MFI in the event of difficulties, for information sharing and to compare notes with regard to outcomes and impact.

Engagement with poor people within the community

The community would need to engage with MFIs in demonstrating how they represent poor people's needs concerning appropriate financial services.

Object motives

There must be a level of mutuality in the outcomes of the MFI and community. Therefore, the object motive would need to be a good fit at the first line of interaction (see discussion above).

The microfinance dialogue space must recognise the interaction of microfinance and communities as two activity systems coming together for mutual outcomes. Their coming together would also recognise that the activity systems would have other outcome expectations that might not concern the collaborating activity system. For example, the sustainability of a microfinance institution need not concern the community or, conversely, how the community ensures its members food and shelter would not concern the microfinance institution.

Responding to Poor People's Voices

In the first chapter Jenala is arguing her case that, as women, they are strong and willing to work but do not have the kind of leadership that would help them. This research journey identified several aspects that would move the conversation for Jenala and other community members who find themselves in poverty.

Considering the research findings, this chapter discusses implications of the theory of dialogue space in microfinance for:

- microfinance institutions;
- communities living in poverty;
- churches and faith-based institutions;
- future research;
- my autobiography.

Implications for Microfinance Institutions

Microfinance institutions that desire to demonstrate social returns would need to ensure that they respond appropriately to the financial needs of target communities. The impact they seek will have to emanate from knowing that their products and services represent a solution for the financial needs of target communities. That would only be possible through dialogue. The research findings highlighted the limitations that communities like the COSUN group would experience to relate their livelihood needs to financial services, even where dialogue space is provided. The research recommends the need for a community dialogue space that would enable poor people to articulate their livelihood needs and, within that context, enable a representation of those needs that require financial services as a solution. In analysing communities as activity systems, microfinance institutions will have a more holistic understanding of the community dynamics in relation to meeting livelihood needs and therefore how financial services could be a solution.

Redefining Social Impact

The theory of dialogue space recognises the scope to which microfinance institutions have to interact with the communities they serve at the point of intersection between those financial solutions and the needs they satisfy in poor people's lives. Provision of those services to meet the financial needs of poor people does constitute a social impact and microfinance institutions can directly collect data through routine work and measure the extent of that impact. A once-removed level of impact is how those financial solutions contribute to the livelihoods of poor people through activities like paying school fees, paying for basic needs like food and shelter, and generally improving their livelihoods. At this level microfinance institutions do not have direct interaction with clients and would have to depend on collaborative dialogue in the microfinance dialogue space. Therefore, microfinance institutions need to redefine their impact-evaluation instruments to recognise the first level where there is direct impact in relation to the actual provision of financial services. An additional level of impact on poor people's lives must come out of collaboration with community dialogue interactions.

A Different Way of Listening – Activity Theory in Practice

Responding to poor people's voices entails listening first. The findings highlighted the interlocutory limitations that poor people have. The implication of that is that microfinance institutions must listen differently. The availability of dialogue spaces in the community implies some level of competent leadership to represent community needs in search of solutions, and this research recommends that it is these leaders that microfinance institutions need to interact with to respond with appropriate financial services. Creating community dialogue spaces would be beyond the purview of microfinance institutions to organise and manage; therefore, they would have to consider partnering with community structures that are housing or have the capacity to create community dialogue spaces to enable useful information for appropriate services. Some rural communities have strong traditional and hereditary ties and can generate robust social capital to enable fruitful engagement within itself. Given the experiences of the COSUN women, it is unlikely that the CPSCC leaders would generate that level of social capital. This leaves urban communities in a dilemma unless a different structure can be employed. The other recognised structure is the Church, whose engagement would need to be explored.

Where dialogue space has enabled progressive interaction with targeted communities, attributing impact would include a collaborative effort between the microfinance institutions and community organisations. The collaborative effort would happen at the level where the use of financial services has enabled livelihood changes. Microfinance institutions would not have a direct view at this level but can collaborate with community organisations to glean information coming out of the community dialogue spaces on the efficacy of the services provided. Thus, microfinance institutions can factor that into their interactions with communities so that together there is agreement on the type of impact sought, how to measure it and at what intervals.

Implications for Communities Living in Poverty

Creation of Community Dialogue Spaces in the Activity Systems

It is important for communities to build these dialogue spaces to facilitate listening to community members, especially poor people, in identifying the livelihood needs. The lack of competent knowledge and skills limitations have serious ramifications for individual and collective agency. However, where communities have organised themselves and community dialogue spaces are functional, the likelihood of there being leadership with the capacity to identify livelihood needs will be high. Once the livelihood needs are known, the quest for solutions will lead to engaging other activity systems like microfinance institutions for solutions to livelihood needs.

As community dialogue spaces enable an understanding of needs and relevant financial services, those conversations can form the basis for determining the types of impact sought through the preferred interventions, and how to measure them. The following is envisioned:

Evaluation of Impact

	Needs	Possible evaluation mechanism
Microfinance Dialogue Space		
Microfinance institutions	1. Institutional sustainability 2. Outreach	- Determine how products should be designed to respond to MFI triple goals and community needs - Determine type of impact expected in line with MFI's mission and community needs - Determine type of instruments to be used to measure impact
	Client impact	
Communities	Financial services to meet needs of the communities: access to credit; access to safe savings mechanisms; insurance and money transmission services	
Community Dialogue Space		
Community members	- What are the livelihood needs? - What financial services are needed? - How is the need for financial services going to be met?	1. Determine how effective the solution was in meeting livelihood needs in the community; 2. Evaluate if it was the right solution for the articulated need; 3. Determine depth of impact and how to measure it 4. Expansive learning for both the community and MFI

Thinking Long-Term Solutions

Communities would need to think about whether and when microfinance can be a useful poverty-reduction tool. The dialogue space in the Chinyika community enabled short-term redress of their problem and engaged in seeking a long-term solution that brought a new way of knowing. Communities should consider more sustainable propositions while evaluating the advantages and disadvantages of employing microfinance as a poverty-reduction strategy. Other strategies like the one the Chinyika community used could serve the community much better than facilitating poor people to go into debt through microfinance loans.

Participation in the Groups – Gender Relations

The freedom to participate implies that participants are fully aware of what it is they are participating in, how that participation will happen and that there are agreed incentives for participation. Participation cannot be assumed but has to be intentionally engrained in the community structures in order to benefit even the most marginalised. There is often a high likelihood of women being taken advantage of where structures do not deliberately recognise their roles and support their efforts. This is more so when women take up the role of leadership in families. Community structures need to deliberately recognise the different gender roles and support women against vulnerability.

Christian Principles for Listening to Poor People

The research findings have implications for Christians. For them, responding to poor people's needs must be steeped in empowering processes that do not marginalise them further. These processes need to engender a sense that poor people's voices are potent and can influence actions that affect them. In their desire to provide a differentiated service, Christian microfinance institutions might need to consider the extent to which they listen to and allow poor people's voices to inform beneficial financial services. From the research findings, some fundamental principles to listening and responding to poor people emerged:

- Poor people know their livelihood needs and can articulate them. Interventions to help them should therefore consider the influence of their voices.
- Poor people often lack competent knowledge to navigate livelihood solutions and need strong support structures to enable them speak and be heard to the extent of their competence.
- Poor people should be facilitated to inform livelihood strategies that benefit them.
- Poor people tend to be marginalised and that increases their vulnerability. They should therefore be given preference in developmental issues that affect them.
- Poor people have the capacity for expansive learning given the right support. That level of support should therefore be afforded them.

A substantive and differentiated approach to listening might mean purposefully partnering with community organisations that oversee or have the capacity to create effective dialogue spaces within the community, and pay special attention to listening to poor people's voices.

The Church is a repository of social capital, necessary for community cohesion. The theological premise recognises God's concern for the marginalised: poor people, the weak and destitute, which is a constant theme echoed by the prophets and particularly evident in Jesus' teachings. The Church's object motive in development work is to ensure the ideal of abundant life as God intended and that the community transformation stories can become part of the story of God's redemptive work in the world. Thus, the Christian Church remains a viable and available option to create dialogue spaces where poor communities could derive support. And this could lead to more inclusive altruistic intents and could begin to deal with the challenge of finding lasting solutions. Microfinance institutions can then partner with such churches or indeed other community organisations with the capacity to open progressive dialogue spaces.

Implications for Future Research

This research has raised several issues that have potential for future research. These are listed and detailed below:

Participatory Action Research for Community and Microfinance Dialogue Spaces

This research identified the need for a microfinance dialogue space that would interact with a community dialogue space to enable appropriate responses with financial services. This research was unable to compel a longer-term dialogue space that could have enabled an understanding of how poor people use the money they borrowed and whether prolonged interactions with them would have identified a different financial solution besides a loan. The dialogue would inform sustainable solutions. The research also recognised the Church as a repository of social capital with potential to bring about transformative solutions to the poverty context. A potential research process would involve the Church providing leadership to create community dialogue spaces. Such research would then interact with microfinance institutions in another dialogue space to inform appropriate responses to poor people's financial needs.

> *Research concern 1: How can the Church position itself in the community as a repository of social capital to sustain progressive dialogue spaces that would inform microfinance practice for appropriate financial services?*

> *Research concern 2: How can communities participate and inform impact assessments based on the content of community dialogue spaces that enable identification of financial needs?*

Facilitating Accumulation of Savings in Lieu of Loans

The COSUN women were saving with CPSCC, where the safety was not known or assured. If one considers that a loan is an aggregation of many small savings that poor people can make, one starts to see the possibilities of the COSUN women being facilitated to accumulate their money in savings to meet their financial needs without the burden of a debt represented by the loan. In this regard, it makes sense that a secure savings product is something that might serve them better. However, those assumptions would need to be supported by an informed assessment.

> **Research concern 3:** *How can poor people be facilitated to accumulate savings securely as a community-driven initiative to meet their livelihood needs?*

Research on Understanding Urban Livelihoods

I was confident that there was a lot more that happened in the COSUN women's lives that would not be revealed in the type of research I had pursued. The COSUN women were in a cash economy with no skills to improve their livelihoods. Yet they had managed to navigate their difficult spaces to eke out a living over time. This is a potential area for future research.

> **Research concern 4:** *How poor people in deprived urban contexts manage to support their livelihoods.*

Implications for my Autobiography

I started this research to address my increasing concern that microfinance practitioners had not engaged poor people adequately enough to understand their specific financing needs to provide appropriate products and services. My curiosity regarding whether the pre-designed financial services were meeting the financial needs of poor people led me to this research process. The research highlighted several issues that have altered my views regarding listening to poor people for improved financial services.

I realised that some of my assumptions did not align with poor people's realities. My thinking was challenged. During the pre-loan meetings most of the women expressed a lack of business skills and, from that point of view, could not inform a business conversation. Consequently, I was not able to figure out the real benefit that the loan had on business efforts; whether they made any profits and whether those profits were adequate to pay back the loan, sustain a livelihood and plough back into the business. Then they stopped meeting after they got the loans, suggesting that they had not seen as much value in the subsequent meetings as in utilising the loan. In my mind, it is the subsequent meetings that would have generated information to inform appropriate products. The meetings would also have enabled a dialogue that clarifies product expectations so that the women would have understood why microfinance institutions structured products the way they did.

From the research I could not see how we as microfinance practitioners could respond appropriately to poor people's financial needs while ensuring organisational sustainability. As an external person to target communities, I did not have the recognised authority to compel actions that would eventually be transformative. I was unable to prevail over the women to continue coming for meetings after they got the loan, even though the leaders had endorsed my presence in that community and I am fully Zambian and therefore consider myself local. The interaction with the Chinyika community made me aware of the importance of community support that is selfless and committed to long-term solutions for communities. In urban settings where disparate ethnicity calls for a different type of community cohesion, I see the Church as having potential to galvanise social capital to enable poor people to navigate their way out of poverty.

Views on Entrepreneurship

I also realised that my thinking that credit was utilised for progressive economic activities was misplaced. I began to understand that a good number of microfinance clients might be in the same position as some of the COSUN women: doing business was a necessary but not a preferred choice. What the women needed was a way of managing the risks associated with not having a regular income. They therefore used the loan money the best way they knew how and returned it as soon as they could. My understanding of entrepreneurship was based on identifying a business opportunity and exploiting it for a financial return. I wondered whether the advent of microfinance loan schemes may have been perceived as yet another donor-driven external intervention. As I reflected on the developments in the Chinyika analysis, I felt that the COSUN women were recipients of help, whereas the Chinyika community were participants in their own development. This would be an impediment to informing financial services that benefit poor people.

Responding to Poor People's Voices

The COSUN case demonstrated the powerlessness associated with poverty. The women were simply not heard; they could not influence decisions that affect them. Trying to respond to their voices in that state would be a futile exercise as those voices have been thwarted. I remained unsure as to whether anyone with authority in that community was aware that some voices had been thwarted and whether they would do something about it. Until that was done, responding to the voices of poor people might remain a pipedream. This research recommended that, in communities with disparate cultural values and norms, community structure would need to be identified to undertake leadership and on-going analysis of the community with a view to ensuring effective dialogue spaces. The Church is one such appropriate entity. Other community organisations could be considered.